Joseph Andrews

A comedy
from the novel by HENRY FIELDING

P. M. CLEPPER

SAMUEL   FRENCH

LONDON
NEW YORK   TORONTO   SYDNEY   HOLLYWOOD

Copyright © 1978 By Patrick Michael Clepper

JOSEPH ANDREWS is fully protected under the copyright laws of the British Commonwealth, including Canada, the United States of America, and all other countries of the Copyright Union. All rights, including professional and amateur stage productions, recitation, lecturing, public reading, motion picture, radio broadcasting, television and the rights of translation into foreign languages are strictly reserved.

ISBN 978-0-573-12209-6

www.samuelfrench-london.co.uk

www.samuelfrench.com

FOR AMATEUR PRODUCTION ENQUIRIES

UNITED KINGDOM AND WORLD
EXCLUDING NORTH AMERICA

plays@SamuelFrench-London.co.uk

020 7255 4302/01

Each title is subject to availability from Samuel French,

depending upon country of performance.

CAUTION: Professional and amateur producers are hereby warned that JOSEPH ANDREWS is subject to a licensing fee. Publication of this play does not imply availability for performance. Both amateurs and professionals considering a production are strongly advised to apply to the appropriate agent before starting rehearsals, advertising, or booking a theatre. A licensing fee must be paid whether the title is presented for charity or gain and whether or not admission is charged.

The professional rights in this play are controlled by Eric Glass Ltd, 25 Ladbroke Crescent, London W11 1PS

No one shall make any changes in this title for the purpose of production. No part of this book may be reproduced, stored in a retrieval system, or transmitted in any form, by any means, now known or yet to be invented, including mechanical, electronic, photocopying, recording, videotaping, or otherwise, without the prior written permission of the publisher. No one shall upload this title, or part of this title, to any social media websites.

The right of HENRY FIELDING and P.M. CLEPPER to be identified as author of this work has been asserted by them in accordance with Section 77 of the Copyright, Designs and Patents Act 1988.

CHARACTERS

Joseph Andrews, a young man whose virtue is endangered
Parson Adams, honest and gullible
Lady Booby, a lusty widow
Fanny, a country maiden
Pamela, she makes virtue pay off
Nephew, he paid, with a wedding ring
Slipslop, lady-in-waiting—waiting for a man
Betty, young servant at an inn; good-hearted
Didapper, would-be seducer
Mrs Tow-Wouse, suspicious inn-keeper
Mrs Trulliber, much like the pigs she raises
Mrs Wilson, narrator—and someone's mother!
Mrs Andrews, nice country-woman
Justice Frolick, justice can be bought
Constable, the law!
Gypsy, your fortune told, anyone?
Female Robber, you can't trust anybody
Male Robber, bit part
Pigs, well, actors have to start somewhere!

The action of the play takes place in Lady Booby's mansion, an inn, the countryside, and elsewhere

Period—about 1740

JOSEPH ANDREWS

A classic comedy, now a major motion picture with Ann-Margret and Peter Firth. Here is an opportunity to put it on your stage in an easy, rollicking version in two acts, for 7 men and 11 women (plus, if you like, a pig-pen of oinkers!). Racy, robust, rowdy, riotous farce from the pen of Henry Fielding, considered the first great novelist, creator of *Tom Jones*. This is his satire on "virtue in peril"—but in this case, it is a young virtuous male who is being pursued, and who tries to keep his honour unsullied for the lovely maiden he wants to marry. Pure Joseph must protect himself against a bevy of high- and low-born females in eighteenth-century England. Each would have him be no better than he should be. In the spoof are such well-drawn characters as Parson Adams, a sort of plump Don Quixote of a clergyman, who gets involved with pigs and with rescuing damsels in distress. And there's Lady Booby, a lively widow who tries her best to stoop to conquer her handsome footman. This script provides a lively Hogartian picture of earthy action and laughter. While relatively simple to stage, it is full of challenges for a wide range of acting skills.

NOTES ON CHARACTERS AND COSTUMES

JOSEPH ANDREWS: A handsome lad of about twenty. He is a wide-eyed innocent. His charm keeps some of his "holier than thou" sentiments from seeming priggish. In the first scenes, he should, if possible, have livery or a nice outfit. Then a travelling cloak. After being robbed, he wears ordinary clothes—shirt and pants that buckle below the knee. At the end, nice clothes of the period, and a night-shirt. He must have a birthmark, in the shape of a strawberry, on his chest.

PARSON ADAMS: About fifty, portly. He is easily taken in by people, but is brave and honest. Fielding says that though he is "a poor parson, he would be bold to say he is an honest man, and would do no ill thing to be made a bishop". He has a habit of snapping his fingers, especially at moments of emotion or crisis. He wears clerical garb, black—perhaps a tattered cassock. He could carry a cane or walking-stick.

LADY BOOBY: "A woman of gaiety, blest with a town education, who spoke of her country neighbours as brutes." She is a widow just past the first blush of youth, but still very much in full bloom, and with an eye to young men. She is rich, and dresses as such. She should probably have at least three changes of costume, starting with a black widow's dress and bonnet; a travelling costume for a visit to Didapper's house, and a fine gown for the last scenes, after her nephew's wedding.

FANNY: A pretty girl of eighteen or so. At first, she wears a maid's costume, then that of a milk-maid on a farm, a night-gown, and a nice dress.

PAMELA: In her twenties, beautiful, innocent-looking, but really an ultra-flirt, which we gather from the way in which she licks her lips, pouts, and arranges her clothes, supposedly decorously, but which shows off her curves. At the beginning, she wears a servant dress, at the end a beautiful wedding gown.

NEPHEW: Country squire in his twenties. He pursues Pamela until she catches him. Good clothes throughout the play, especially at the end, when he is a bridegroom.

SLIPSLOP: A waiting-gentlewoman, daughter of a clergyman, thus above the other servants, but below the gentry. She is described as "forty-five, short, rather fat, not remarkably handsome". She is not too far gone to desire Joseph. She holds her station because she knows all the family secrets, much of this information being gathered by eavesdropping. Her clothes befit her station—neither poor nor rich.

DIDAPPER: He attempts to be a "beau", a dandy. The author calls him "four-foot-five, thin and pale, he more hops than walks—this little thing". Dresses gaudily. Night-gown for bedroom scene.

MRS TOW-WOUSE: Running a public inn has toughened her. "Short, thin and crooked. Chin peaked. Her lips are two bits of skin, which, whenever she spoke, she drew together in a purse. Small red eyes. Voice both loud and hoarse." Wears plain dress, with perhaps an apron and cap.

MRS TRULLIBER: She raises pigs, and is large, with a loud voice. She is said to walk like a goose. She wears old, dirty clothes, with an apron.

BETTY: A servant in the Dragon Inn. Pretty. She wears drab clothes, and a cloak.

MRS WILSON: A refined country gentlewoman, nicely dressed.

MRS ANDREWS: Another nice country woman, but poor, and dresses as such.

JUSTICE FROLICK: Probably middle-aged or elderly. Wears black judicial robes, and a powdered wig, and could carry a gavel, if desired.

CONSTABLE: Could be almost any age from twenties to sixties. Rough, tough. He might wear some sort of ragtag uniform coat and hat to show his office, and he might carry a club. He carries a rope looped in his belt.

GYPSY: Older woman, who could dress in a stereotyped way—colourful dress, with bandanna on her head, and lots of gaudy bracelets, rings, and necklaces.

FEMALE ROBBER: Any age. Tough. Lower-class, dark clothes.

MALE ROBBER: Same as for her.

PIGS: The pig farm scene could be done without pigs, but if they are used, they could be actors—whatever age, including young children—dressed in either realistic costumes or very stylized. They act in a comical way when Parson Adams tries to grab them, and falls among them.

There might also be a stylized cow for the scene in the dairy barn with Fanny.

STAGING SUGGESTIONS

The faster the action moves, the better. Therefore, the settings should either be very simple, or designed for swift changes.

A plain stage probably is best, with props and furniture denoting a setting rather than fully furnishing it.

The Booby mansion parlour might be represented by a few good chairs and a settee, on which Lady Booby could recline.

Later, the sleeping quarters of the Booby mansion are represented by two beds. If possible, these should show some elegance, such as canopies.

Without the canopy, one of them might be the bed in the Dragon Inn, in which Joseph is placed after the robbery.

The inn setting might have a bar, with glasses, and some benches. Perhaps a sign hung some place could proclaim, "Dragon Inn".

Many of the scenes are played with no settings or props, such as Joseph's robbery, and Nephew's interview with Justice Frolick.

Several of the scenes are played in dimness, so that the audience can accept the fact that the characters cannot be identified, such as Fanny's attempted ravishment, and the bedroom scene near the end.

Indications (L and R) have been provided for entrances and exits in certain instances—but these are expendable, and the director and/or the actors may come up with ones that are more suitable to a particular staging.

ACT I*

The Parlour of the Booby mansion

Mrs Wilson is narrator as well as a character in the play. For her introductory remarks to the audience, she might either go in front of the CURTAIN, *or if there is no* CURTAIN, *enter* R *into the set. She uses an appropriate greeting—*
"Good evening", "Good afternoon", or "Good morning"

Mrs Wilson Good evening. My name is Mrs Wilson. (*As if someone in the audience did not hear, and asked*) Mrs Wilson. I am here to tell you a story. It is not about me. If I told you some of what has happened to me, it might bring tears. But that belongs to the past, decades ago, when our country got a monarch from Hanover, George the First, after William and Mary were both gone—the turn of a century, into the eighteenth. But no tears for me. *This* story is mostly full of laughter. It happened in the part of England in which I live. There is a huge mansion and estate that belonged to Sir Thomas Booby—yes, that's correct, Sir Thomas Booby—the *late* Sir Thomas. He is now gone two or three weeks—still very much grieved by everyone—even at times by his widow. Not too often. In that mighty mansion is a servant, Pamela.

Pamela enters L, *closely followed by Nephew. She flirts and poses prettily as she pretends to work, such as straightening furniture*

Mrs Wilson Pamela is a demure young lass, who is sought after by the nephew of the house—Lady Booby's nephew. He will seek in vain until he comes forth with a wedding ring—for Pamela is ambitious. She aims for a place far above the station to which she was born. (*She stands and watches*)
Nephew O Pamela, dearest Pamela, my dearest Pamela, my . . .
Pamela O please, sir. I have my work to do.
Nephew I have my pleasure to do.
Pamela O sir, attractive as you are, I dare not lift my eyes so high. I am only a poor servant girl, and I fear you trifle with me.
Nephew I *would* trifle, if you allowed me.
Pamela La, what would you have me do? I am only a servant here in your aunt's home. And I must do my work to please her. Else, she will cast me out, and I would never see you again.
Nephew Nor I you.
Pamela So, I must do my work to her satisfaction. And I must please her in my person. Do you think the shoulder of this dress is sewn correctly? It looks different than the other, doesn't it? (*She postures*)
Nephew It looks the same to me. And the shoulder—divine!
Pamela O sir, you are making sport of a poor unmarried little country maiden.

---

* Paragraph 3 on page ii of this Acting Edition regarding photocopying and videorecording should be carefully read.

Pretending dismay, Pamela runs off R

Nephew O my dearest, gorgeous, delectable Pamela.

Nephew exits R

During the following, Lady Booby and Adams enter L. *She is in mourning clothes, and carries a prayer-book*

Mrs Wilson After church this morning, Lady Booby is accompanied home by Parson Adams. One of the kindest men alive. Learned in books, the good clergyman knows nothing of the world and its people. He cannot see through a child, much less the devious persons that fill all ranks of society.
Lady Booby Thank you, parson. It was kind of you to escort me home.
Adams I thought you will need guidance in your hour of grief.
Lady Booby *Hour* of grief? It's been at least half-a-year.
Adams Only a few weeks, Lady Booby.
Lady Booby Is that all the longer I've been bereaved? (*Looking down at her clothes*) I am thoroughly sick of black.
Adams (*scandalized*) Madam! I must tell you that when I was preaching this morning, I thought you looked—well, indifferent. When I was praising your late husband, you seemed—bored.
Lady Booby Parson Adams, you did not read my expression correctly. I try stoically to restrain any outward show of my grief, not to let the general populace see me shattered. For them, I must be a steadfast example.
Adams (*taken in*) Of course! O Lady Booby, forgive me. How brave—not to wish to burden others with your great sorrow.
Lady Booby Yes, that's it, Parson Adams—my bravery. And now I must rest.
Adams I know, Lady Booby, you wish to commune with your soul and with your husband.
Lady Booby What?
Adams The spirit of your late and lamented . . .
Lady Booby O yes, that is what I am going to do, parson—commune with spirits. Please allow me to invite you to go to the kitchen, and have yourself some tea, or whatever it is that will refresh you.
Adams Your ladyship is most kind.

Adams bows out R

Lady Booby throws down the prayer-book and bonnet

Lady Booby (*bellowing*) Mrs Slipslop. Slipslop!
Mrs Wilson Mrs Slipslop, Lady Booby's lady-in-waiting and housekeeper.

Slipslop enters L

Act I 3

Slipslop Ma'am?
Lady Booby Slipslop, after my ordeal in church—my grief being renewed by the reminder of . . .
Slipslop (*knowingly*) O yes, your grief.
Lady Booby A little wine. It might help. A sip. A taste. A little glass.
Slipslop A tumbler.
Lady Booby And Slipslop, I know you are over-worked, so don't go to the trouble of bringing it yourself. Have you-know-who serve it to me.
Slipslop Yes, ma'am, you'll-know-who-then will bring it.

Slipslop exits R

Mrs Booby reclines, her eyes closed

Mrs Wilson "You-know-who" is Joseph Andrews. Joey is a handsome young footman. And he is, by-the-by, the brother of that saucy little flirt, Pamela. Mrs Slipslop knows who Lady Booby wants—Joseph to bring her the refreshment—but being Slipslop, impertinent Mrs Slipslop, she sends Fanny Goodwill.

Fanny enters R *with a tray on which are a decanter of wine and a large glass*

Lady Booby is relaxing with her eyes closed

Mrs Wilson Having Fanny here will infuriate Lady Booby, as Slipslop knows.

Mrs Wilson exits R

Lady Booby Is that you, Joseph? O, I need what you have to bring to me.
Fanny Lady Booby, it is me, Fanny.
Lady Booby (*indignantly, opening her eyes*) Fanny? I wanted—I'm surprised the two of you didn't carry it in together, he's always so close to you.
Fanny Joseph? Ma'am, there has been no impropriety.
Lady Booby Did I say there was? Do you reveal a guilty conscience? Denying what only you know should be denied?
Fanny Yes, ma'am. I mean, no, ma'am.
Lady Booby You don't know what you mean, that's what you mean. O the lower classes! You should be forever grateful to this noble family, the Boobys.
Fanny (*who has heard it all before*) Yes, ma'am. May I . . .
Lady Booby (*going on with her story*) My father-in-law bought you from a travelling-woman—a gypsy, Fanny, a gypsy!
Fanny Yes, ma'am. Will there be . . .
Lady Booby (*getting up*) The gypsies stole you from heaven knows where. You were only three or four years old. I believe they had you for

several years, then decided to sell you. And they were paid three guineas —a fortune—for you, you ungrateful miss, who now ...
Fanny I'm not ungrate ...
Lady Booby (*interrupting*) They said you were almost impossible to describe, you were such a beautiful young creature. Hmm? If that was true, how came you to be so plain now? Though I suppose Joseph Andrews, as well as other men of the servant class, might be so blind as to think you, well, passable.
Fanny (*setting down the tray*) Joseph does say that ...
Lady Booby Enough of your idle patter, you vain strumpet. Wait until I get my claws at that Slipslop for sending you with the wine! (*She opens several buttons at the neck of her dress to cool down, as she strides off*)

Lady Booby exits L. *Adams enters* R

Adams Ah, Fanny, how are you?
Fanny As ever, parson. I don't know how I'm to please any in this house.
Adams (*slyly*) Any *women*, that is.
Fanny Parson Adams, please say that you will wed me.
Adams My dear girl, I *am* married.
Fanny No, no, I mean, say that you will wed me to Joseph Andrews.
Adams Fanny, as I have told you all the other times you two have asked me, I cannot in good conscience.
Fanny But ...
Adams Wait a few years.
Fanny Years! It's a long time to wait if you're young.
Adams I know. But with a few years of service here, and you thrifty with your wages, then you will be able to live comfortably.
Fanny I don't care about being comfortable—I want to be married.

Slipslop enters R

Adams (*leaving*) Good-day.

Adams exits L

Fanny Mrs Slipslop ...
Slipslop Get about your work.
Fanny The other servants tell me that you want to send me to the farm to live. Why, Mrs Slipslop, why?
Slipslop It is my job as general housekeeper to see that the work is done well.
Fanny Has her ladyship complained of my work?
Slipslop Do you think her ladyship has nothing better to do than see how well you do your work—or *don't* do it?
Fanny I do my work, Mrs Slipslop.

Act I

Slipslop Don't argue with me, you young snip. I have been observing you, and I think you fit well in a cow barn than in the house of gentry.
Fanny (*tearfully*) Then they are right.
Slipslop Right? Who is right about what?
Fanny The other servants. They told me that . . .
Slipslop That what, hussy? What tittle-tattle?
Fanny That you'd try to send me away because—because . . .
Slipslop Because?
Fanny Because I am pretty, and you . . .
Slipslop (*spluttering and stumbling, she is so incensed*) And me? I—they—you think you—your supposed prettiness puts *me* in the shade?
Fanny Her ladyship won't do it—send me away—just because you say I don't do my work.
Slipslop Then I'll tell her more.
Fanny Tell her more? More what? It'll be more than you know is true of me then.
Slipslop You damn jade. How dare the likes of you . . . Out, out! I'll see to it you get sent to the farm. Out!
Fanny (*calling*) Joseph, Joseph!

Fanny continues to call as she runs out R, *chased by Slipslop*

At the same time, we hear Lady Booby calling

Lady Booby (*off*) Joseph, Joseph Andrews! Joseph, I say.

Lady Booby enters L, *just as Joseph enters* R

Lady Booby Joseph! There you are at last.
Joseph Is everyone calling for me at once?
Lady Booby I don't answer for everybody—I am me, your ladyship.
Joseph Yes, your ladyship. How may I serve you?
Lady Booby (*intrigued by the possibilities*) Well, I—I want you to pour me a glass of wine.
Joseph (*puzzled*) Pour a—Lady Booby?
Lady Booby Yes. Is that so difficult to comprehend?
Joseph No, madam. (*He pours*)
Lady Booby O Joseph, you pour so gently, so genteely, so smoothly. I hate the rude splashes when others do it.
Joseph Yes, madam.
Lady Booby (*taking the glass*) Pray, Joseph, answer me this question. Suppose a lady should happen to like you. Suppose she should prefer you to all your sex, and admit you to the same familiarities as you might have hoped for if you had been born her equal. Can you keep a secret, my Joey?
Joseph Yes, madam.
Lady Booby (*looking down at her open neck*) La! What am I doing? I have trusted myself with a man alone, practically undressed.

Joseph (*blushing*) You're not un . . .

Lady Booby Suppose you should have wicked intentions on my honour. How should I defend myself?

Joseph I never had the least evil design against you, madam.

Lady Booby No, perhaps *you* may not call your designs wicked . . .

Joseph I swear they are not.

Lady Booby If they are against my honour, they may not be wicked, but the world calls them so. But then, say you, the world will never know anything of the matter. Yet, would that not be trusting to your secrecy? Must not my reputation be then in your power? Would you not then be my master?

Joseph I had rather die a thousand deaths than give you any reason to suspect me.

Lady Booby But I have reason to suspect you. Are you not a man? And, without vanity, I may pretend to some charms. You know, Joey, I am of a forgiving temper. Tell me, Joey, don't you think I should forgive you?

Joseph Indeed, madam, I will never do anything to disoblige your ladyship.

Lady Booby (*upbraidingly*) How do you think it would not disoblige me then? Do you think I would willingly suffer you to . . . ?

Joseph I don't understand you, madam.

Lady Booby Don't you? Get you gone. Your pretended innocence cannot impose on me.

Joseph Madam, I would not have your ladyship think any evil of me. I have always endeavoured to be a dutiful servant to you and the master.

Lady Booby O thou villain! Why didst thou mention that dear man, unless to torment me, to bring his precious memory to my mind.

Joseph But madam, a thousand times you wished him dead.

Outraged, Lady Booby exits L. *Slipslop enters* R. *She goes to Joseph to "fix" his clothes and hair—anything to be near him and fondle him.*

Slipslop I overheard it all. Sure nothing can be a more simple contract in a woman than to place her affections on a boy. If I thought it would have been my fate, I should have wished to die a thousand deaths rather than live to see that day. If we like a *man*, the lightest hint sophisticates. Whereas a *boy* propose upon us to break through all the regulations of modesty, before we can make any oppression upon him.

Joseph (*who has been increasingly puzzled by her words*) Yes, madam.

Slipslop (*heatedly*) Yes, madam! Do you intend to result my passion? Is it not enough, ungrateful that you are, to make no return to all the favours I have done you, but you must treat me with ironing? Barbarous monster! How have I deserved that my passion should be resulted and treated with ironing?

Joseph Madam, I don't understand your hard words, but I am certain you have no occasion to call me ungrateful, for, so far from intending you

Act I 7

any wrong, I have always loved you as well as if you had been my own mother.
Slipslop Your mother? Do you assinuate that I am old enough to be your mother? Your mother?

Lady Booby enters L. *Joseph hurries off* R

Lady Booby I am afraid Joseph Andrews is a wild young fellow.
Slipslop That he is, and a wicked one, too. To my knowledge he games, drinks, swears, and fights eternally.

Lady Booby is not interested in this, and drinks placidly: so Slipslop goes a step further

Besides, he is horribly indicted for wenching.
Lady Booby (*interested*) Wenching? Ay! I never heard that of him.
Slipslop O madam. He is so lewd a rascal that if your ladyship keep him much longer, you will not have one virgin in your house—except myself.
Lady Booby Which of the women do you most suspect?
Slipslop Madam, there is Fanny, the chambermaid. I am almost convicted that she is with child by him.
Lady Booby Ay! Then pray pay her her wages instantly. I will keep no sluts in my house. And as for Joseph—send him to me.
Slipslop (*going*) Yes, your ladyship.

Slipslop exits R

Lady Booby finishes her drink in a gulp, then quickly pours herself another glass, and goes to the settee and languishes

Joseph enters R

Joseph You wished to see me, madam?
Lady Booby Joseph, I am sorry to hear such complaints against you.
Joseph Complaints, ma'am? Against me?
Lady Booby I am told you behave so rudely to the maids that they cannot do their business in quiet. I mean those who are not wicked enough to hearken to your solicitions. As to the others, they may, perhaps, not call you rude, for there are wicked sluts who make one ashamed of one's own sex, and are as ready to admit any nauseous familiarity as fellows to offer it.
Joseph But I . . .
Lady Booby Come hither, Joseph. Another mistress might discard you for these offences. But I have a compassion for your youth, and if I could be certain you would be no more guilty . . . (*She puts her hand carelessly on his*)
Joseph Madam, by all that is sacred, I have never offered more than kissing.

Lady Booby Kissing! Do you call that no crime? Kissing, Joseph, is as a prologue to a play. Can I believe a young fellow of your age and complexion will be content with kissing? No, Joseph, there is no woman who grants that but will grant more. And I am deceived greatly in you if you would not put her closely to it. What would you think, Joseph, if I admitted you to kiss me?

Joseph I would sooner die than have any such thought.

Lady Booby And yet, Joseph, ladies have admitted their footmen to such familiarities. And footmen, I confess to you, much less deserving them—fellows without half your charms—for such might almost excuse the crime. Tell me therefore, Joseph, if I should admit you to such freedom, what would you think of me? Tell me freely.

Joseph Madam . . .

Lady Booby Would not you insist on more? Would you be contented with a kiss? Would not your inclinations be all on fire by such a favour?

Joseph Madam, if they were, I hope I should be able to control them, without suffering them to get the better of my virtue.

Lady Booby Your virtue! Your virtue! Intolerable confidence! Have you the assurance to pretend that when a lady demeans herself to throw aside the rules of decency, in order to honour you with the highest favour in her power, your *virtue* should resist her inclination? That, when she had conquered her own virtue, she should find an obstruction in yours?

Joseph Madam, I can't see why her having no virtue should be a reason against my having any, or why, because I am a man, or because I am poor, my virtue must be subservient to her pleasure.

Lady Booby I am out of patience! Did ever mortal hear of a *man*'s virtue? Did ever the greatest or gravest man pretend to any of this kind? And can a boy have the confidence to talk of his virtue?

Joseph Madam, that boy is the brother of Pamela, and would be ashamed that the chastity of his family, which is preserved in her, should be stained in him.

Lady Booby You impudent villain! Do you insult me with the follies of my nephew, who hath exposed himself to ridicule all over the country by pursuing your sister? A little vixen. Sirrah! Get out of my sights, and prepare to set out this night, for I will order you your wages immediately. Get out, get out!

Joseph exits L. *Slipslop enters* R. *She has overheard all and is unhappy at this result*

Slipslop, I find too much reason to believe all thou has told me of this wicked Joseph. I have determined to part with him instantly.

Slipslop I am sorry for it, and, if I had known you would have punished the poor lad so severely, you should never have heard a particle of the matter. Here's a fuss indeed about nothing!

Lady Booby Nothing? Do you think I will countenance lewdness in my house?

Act I

Slipslop If you will turn away every footman that is a lover of the sport, you must open the coach door yourself.
Lady Booby Don't shock my ears with your beastly language.
Slipslop Marry-come-up, people's ears are sometimes the nicest part about them.
Lady Booby What is meant by the extraordinary degree of freedom in which you indulge your tongue?
Slipslop Servants have tongues as well as their mistresses.
Lady Booby Yes, and saucy ones too. Unless you mend your manners, this house is no place for you.
Slipslop Manners! I never was thought to want manners nor modesty neither. And for places, there are more places than one. And I know what I know.
Lady Booby What do you know, mistress?
Slipslop I am not obliged to tell that to everybody . . . any more than I am obliged to keep it a secret.
Lady Booby (*getting the drift*) Slipslop, I should be very unwilling to part with you. I believe, likewise, you have found me an indulgent mistress on many occasions, and have as little reason on your side to desire a change.
Slipslop That's true . . . (*She picks up the tray with the decanter and glass*)
Lady Booby I have been meaning to give you a gift or two . . .

Lady Booby and Slipslop exit R. *Pamela enters* L, *with Fanny, Mrs Andrews and Joseph, who is in a travelling-cloak, and carries a small bundle of his belongings*

Mrs Andrews O my son . . .
Joseph Mother—when I was dismissed, I told Mrs Slipslop to give my wages to you.
Mrs Andrews No, no, if you are off on the road. . .
Joseph (*firmly*) The money is for you. You need it more than I will. I can find employment. I will seek it in London. Good-bye, Mother.
Mrs Andrews Good-bye, son, and may God take care of you.

Mrs Andrews exits L

Joseph Pamela . . .
Pamela How awful to be sent away like this. With such pitiful little money and worldly goods.
Joseph O most adorable sister. Most virtuous sister—whose example could alone enable me to withstand all the temptations of riches and beauty, and to preserve my virtue pure and chaste for the arms of my dear Fanny!
Fanny O Joseph dearest.
Joseph What riches and honours or pleasures can make us amends for the loss of innocence? Doth not that alone afford us more consolation than all wordly acquisitions?

Pamela (*thinking this over*) Well-l-l . . . Farewell, my dear brother. Godspeed and a prosperous end to your journey. May you find a good position in London, a *well-paying* position.

Pamela and Joseph wave to each other

Pamela exits R

Joseph (*to Fanny*) O thou delightful charming creature! If we could afford to be husband and wife! If Heaven had indulged thee in my arms, the poorest, humblest state would have been a paradise. I could have lived with thee in the lowest cottage without envying the palaces, the dainties, or the riches of any man breathing.

Fanny unties from her neck a ribbon on which is a small piece of gold

Fanny Take this with you, Joseph, as a remembrance. It is the little piece of gold that, I'm told, I had with me when I was sold here to this house, so many years ago. I have made a ribbon for it, on which are entwined our names. Wear it and may it remind you of your faithful maid, waiting for you.

Crying, she ties it around his neck. They embrace and kiss, then tearfully break away

Joseph exits R. *Fanny exits* L, *as Mrs Wilson enters* R

Mrs Wilson And so Joseph set out with little money and less hope in search of a bright future.

Mrs Wilson watches as scene changes. Parlour disappears and it is a road

Joseph enters R *as if walking along a road, dejectedly. A Female Robber and Male Robber enter* L *with an old-fashioned hand-gun*

Male Robber Stand.
Joseph What? What is . . . ?
Female Robber Quiet. Give us your money.
Joseph I have—very little.

The Female Robber searches him and gets one of the few coins he has

Male Robber Strip.
Joseph What?
Female Robber We want your clothes. We can sell them.
Joseph But I . . .
Male Robber Strip and be damned to you.
Joseph I can't—not in front of a lady.
Male Robber (*amused*) A lady? Ha!
Female Robber (*to her companion*) Watch your tongue, you pig.
Male Robber Strip, or I'll blow your brains to the devil.

Act I

Joseph The clothes are not worth much. Consider the coldness of the weather.
Male Robber You are cold, are you? (*Waving the pistol*) I'll warm you.

Joseph starts to slowly remove his cloak and other clothes. The Female Robber notices the gold on the ribbon

Female Robber What's that?
Male Robber Gold!
Female Robber I'll have that.
Joseph No! You can have everything but that dear piece of gold. (*He struggles with her*)
Female Robber Give it to me. Let go!
Male Robber I'll make him let go of you, my dear.

He savagely hits Joseph's head with the pistol. Joseph falls unconscious. The Female Robber rips the ribbon from his neck

The Male Robber and Female Robber take most of Joseph's clothes and exit L

Mrs Wilson Joseph was found by a pretty little chambermaid from the nearby inn, called the Dragon. Betty was her name, and a good heart she had.

Mrs Wilson exits L. *Betty enters* R *and sees Joseph*

Betty Who ...? A dead man! (*Going to him*) No, no, not dead, but his head is hurt bad. (*She puts her cloak on him*) Sir, sir, can you hear me? We must get you to the inn where I work. It is nearby. Sir, sir, please wake up.
Joseph (*groggily*) Mercy on me. I have been robbed.
Betty Robbed for sure. You were almost as naked as ever you were born. Can you walk? It isn't far. I'll help you.

Betty gets him on his unsteady feet, and puts his arm around her shoulders for support, while one of her arms is around his waist. The Scene changes. They go to the part of the stage which is the Dragon Inn

Mrs Tow-Wouse enters L *and sees them*

Mrs Tow-Wouse Who's there? Betty?
Betty Yes, Mrs Tow-Wouse.
Mrs Tow-Wouse What is it you have there?
Betty A poor naked man, who has been robbed and murdered.
Mrs Tow-Wouse Robbed?
Betty Of all he had.
Mrs Tow-Wouse Well then, where's his money to pay for his keep here at the inn. We'll send him packing.

Betty sets Joseph down on a bench

Betty Common charity won't suffer you to do that, Mrs Tow-Wouse.

Mrs Tow-Wouse Common charity! Common charity teaches us to provide for ourselves and our families. And I and mine won't be ruined by charity, I assure you.

Betty I tell you, he's in extreme danger of his life.

Mrs Tow-Wouse Here's a pretty kettle of fish you've brought upon us. We are like to have a funeral at our own expense.

Betty If he dies, the parish should be at the expense of the funeral.

Mrs Tow-Wouse That's some consolation, at least.

Betty Not much for him.

Joseph I . . .

Betty Yes, what is it?

Joseph I am dry. May I have a little tea?

Mrs Tow-Wouse I have just done drinking it, and cannot be slopping all day.

Betty You shall have tea, sir, if there is any in the land. (*To Mrs Tow-Wouse*) I never saw a finer skin in my life.

Mrs Tow-Wouse Pox on his skin. I suppose that is all we are like to have for the reckoning.

Joseph Pray, miss . . .

Betty Yes?

Joseph Did you find a little piece of broken gold . . .

Mrs Tow-Wouse Gold? Does he have gold?

Betty I told you he had been robbed. Of course he doesn't have it.

Mrs Tow-Wouse Did you search his clothes?

Betty He had no clothes.

Mrs Tow-Wouse Well!

Joseph I beg you, help me find that little gold piece which has a ribbon tied to it.

Betty We'll try, sir. (*To Mrs Tow-Wouse*) I'll put him to bed.

Mrs Tow-Wouse Don't linger. He has no money, remember.

Betty aids Joseph to the exit L. *Adams enters* R. *He is dressed for journeying, and carries a big back-pack*

Adams Good morning, hostess.

Mrs Tow-Wouse Good morning—a parson, isn't it?

Adams (*good naturedly*) Yes, my cassock gives me away, doesn't it?

Mrs Tow-Wouse A worthy occupation, to be sure, sir. Are you visiting this part of the country?

Adams No, just passing through.

Mrs Tow-Wouse To where?

Adams London.

Mrs Tow-Wouse Ah. A great village, I hear.

Adams Indeed yes.

Mrs Tow-Wouse You have a church there?

Adams No, no. I am a country parson. I am on my way to London to publish three volumes of sermons. (*He pats his back-pack*)
Mrs Tow-Wouse (*unimpressed*) Your sermons—in a book? How marvellous.
Adams Yes. I have been encouraged by an advertisement lately set forth by the society of booksellers, who proposed to purchase any copies offered to them. I imagine I shall get a considerable sum of money, which my family is in urgent need of.
Mrs Tow-Wouse Does that mean you have no money now?
Adams I don't need much. The Lord provides.
Mrs Tow-Wouse But inn-keepers don't.
Adams I have nine shillings and threepence-halfpenny in my pocket.
Mrs Tow-Wouse To get you all the way to London. My, my, you are well provided for, for a journey of that length.

The Female Robber enters R

Mrs Tow-Wouse And what do you want?
Female Robber Some ale. And some food to carry to my friends.
Mrs Tow-Wouse What friends? Where?
Female Robber There is a coach up the road.
Mrs Tow-Wouse Up the road? Why don't they stop here for a decent meal, at a table?
Female Robber You think they want to come here to this rats-nest of an inn?

Betty enters L.

Mrs Tow-Wouse O! Too good for here? You sure you got money?
Female Robber I got something just as good.
Mrs Tow-Wouse There's nothing good as money.
Female Robber There's gold.

Betty becomes alert when she hears the word "gold"

Mrs Tow-Wouse Gold?
Female Robber Yes, gold.
Mrs Tow-Wouse And the likes of you have some? I doubt it.
Female Robber (*taking out Joseph's gold piece on a ribbon*) There!
Mrs Tow-Wouse It *looks* like gold.
Female Robber It *is* gold.
Mrs Tow-Wouse Where did *you* get it?
Female Robber Never you mind. Do you want to do business or don't you?

Betty goes to her

Betty I'll tell you where she got it, Mrs Tow-Wouse. She stole it.
Mrs Tow-Wouse Now, Betty . . .
Female Robber (*with false bravado*) Stole it? How dare . . .

Betty I'll wager that that little piece of gold is the one the young man complained of having stolen from him.

Betty makes a grab for the gold, but the Female Robber quickly gets it out of her reach. Betty grabs her, and they tumble down. There is much screaming, and both Adams and Mrs Tow-Wouse get involved, trying to separate the fighting women. All are rolling around. Adams gets the gold piece

The Female Robber manages to get to her feet and runs off R.

Adams examines the gold and the ribbon

Adams "Joseph—Fanny." Joseph! I do believe this belongs to a friend of mine.
Betty He is here, sir. He was hurt in the robbery. Seriously hurt, though I think he will be all right with a bit of rest.
Mrs Tow-Wouse (*taking the gold from Adams*) The gold belongs to the manor.
Betty How do you figure that, Mrs Tow-Wouse?
Mrs Tow-Wouse The law makes a difference between things stolen and things found.
Adams Yes, but . . .
Mrs Tow-Wouse A thing may be stolen that is never found. And a thing may be found that was never stolen. Now goods that are both stolen and found—belong to the mistress of the manor.
Betty (*taking the gold from her*) So the mistress of the manor is the receiver of stolen goods? (*She turns the gold over to Adams*) Sir, your friend is through there, second door to the left.

Adams exits L.

Betty tries to soothe Mrs Tow-Wouse, who is unhappy about losing the gold

Betty Madam, I believe the man in bed is a greater man than we took him for.
Mrs Tow-Wouse How?
Betty Besides the extreme whiteness of his skin . . .
Mrs Tow-Wouse His soft skin again.
Betty And the softness of his hands—not the hands of a labouring man—observe that this gentleman—(*referring to Adams*)—seems on good terms of familiarity with him. A clergyman, probably from a good parish. Gentleman equals money.
Mrs Tow-Wouse (*thinking this over*) God forbid I should not discharge the duty of a Christian, since the poor gentleman was brought to my house—by providence.
Betty By me, you mean.
Mrs Tow-Wouse If he be a gentleman, we likely will be paid hereafter. Betty, go see what he wants. God forbid he should want anything in my house.

Act I

Betty and Mrs Tow-Wouse exit R

The bed in which Joseph has been placed is either revealed or pushed into place on the stage

Adams enters L *and comes to his side*

Joseph awakes. He is in pain, and puts his hand to his head. Then he notices his visitor, but does not recognize him until he squints and attempts to focus

Adams It is me, Joseph, Parson Adams.
Joseph (*foggily*) Adams? Parson Ad... (*Startled and alert, thinking the parson is bringing bad news*) Parson Adams! How is Fanny? Is she all right?
Adams In perfect health, my young friend. Don't worry about *her* health. How is yours?
Joseph I am very sore.
Adams Do you think you can travel soon?
Joseph I don't know. Must we go now?
Adams (*firmly*) Not until you are fit to go. However, I must own to you that my stock of cash has decreased. It cannot survive another day's bills.
Joseph Then I must arise.
Adams (*pushing him gently back*) Then you must rest and recover. I have luckily many sure methods of obtaining enough for us to live on.

Adams exits L, *passing Betty, who enters. She carries a warming-pan*

Betty Sir, would you like something to warm your bed?
Joseph What?
Betty I have brought a warming-pan, young master.

He does not want her to, but she lifts the covers and begins sensuously warming the bed with the pan

Joseph Please, I don't need... The bed is hot enough. I—I think I have a fever.
Betty You are the handsomest creature I have ever seen! (*She abandons the warming-pan and attempts to wrap him in her arms*) I know a way to reduce that fever! We'll get you sweating.
Joseph (*struggling*) I am sorry to see a young woman cast off her regard for modesty.
Betty Come, come, cast off everything.
Joseph I will cast you off first.
Betty I saved your life.
Joseph I am grateful, but I cannot repay you in this way.
Betty Others think me irresistible, I can tell you.

He wins the struggle, and takes her by the arm

Joseph Thank God a man cannot—like a woman—be ravaged against his will.

Joseph shoves out the taunting and affronted Betty

Betty exits

Joseph returns to his bed and collapses in it, in relief, and primly covers up to go to sleep

The bedroom setting disappears. There appears a dairy setting (with a cow, if desired). Fanny is milking it (or enters R with a pail)

Pamela enters L

Pamela (*calling*) Fanny. Fanny Goodwill. Fanny, I say.
Fanny Here I am. Who—Pamela? What are you doing on the farm?
Pamela I have bad news, Fanny.
Fanny What is it?
Pamela Joseph . . .
Fanny What of my dear Joseph?
Pamela My brother has been robbed and killed, nearly.
Fanny O! O!
Pamela I have been told he is at the Dragon Inn, many miles from here.
Fanny And why are you here? Why are you not with him. You, his sister.
Pamela I cannot go. I must stay to be near . . . Well, if I leave, Lady Booby's nephew perhaps will look elsewhere.
Fanny But Joseph—I must go to him.
Pamela Leave your position here? You can't.
Fanny O, I can! I love your brother with an inexpressible violence. But you should know about love.
Pamela I? How should I know of love?
Fanny You wish to marry Lady Booby's nephew.
Pamela I *will* marry him, but what has that to do with love? Especially my young virgin, this love of "inexpressible violence."
Fanny I mean, of course, with the purest and most delicate passion.
Pamela "Pure passion"—whatever that might be.
Fanny I must hurry to Joseph.

Fanny runs off L, still carrying the pail

Pamela (*calling after, then following*) At least leave the milk-pail.

Pamela exits L

The scene shifts to the Dragon Inn

Act I

Mrs Tow-Wouse enters L, *closely followed by Adams, who is carrying his back-pack*

Adams Mrs Tow-Wouse, dear inn-keeper . . .
Mrs Tow-Wouse (*all affability*) Yes, my dear Parson Adams, what is it I can do for you?
Adams I wish to borrow three guineas.
Mrs Tow-Wouse (*icing up*) Three . . . ! O.
Adams For which I will put ample security into your hands.
Mrs Tow-Wouse Ah. A watch? A ring with a precious stone? What of value is it? What of *double* value is it?
Adams (*indicating his back-pack*) Those sermons I told you of.
Mrs Tow-Wouse Sermons? For security?
Adams There is in that bag no less than nine volumes worth—not three guineas, not thirty—but a hundred pounds at least.
Mrs Tow-Wouse Mr Adams, I have work to . . .
Adams I will deposit one of the volumes in your hands by way of pledge—not doubting but that you will have the honesty to return it on my repayment of the money. For it is worth, just that one volume, ten pounds, as I have been informed by a neighbouring clergymen in the country.
Mrs Tow-Wouse I am no judge of such goods.
Adams Certainly you would not scruple to lend me three guineas on what is undoubtedly . . .
Mrs Tow-Wouse I do not believe I have so much money in the house. (*Pretending to hear someone calling*) Coming, sir. I must go, parson, (*Calling off*) Coming.
Adams What? I heard no one.
Mrs Tow-Wouse Ah, there he is calling again. Impatiently. Excuse me, parson. (*Calling off*) Coming, sir.

Mrs Tow-Wouse exits L

Adams I believe the devil has more humanity. (*He puts his back-pack under the table*)

Slipslop enters R

Slipslop! My dear Mrs Slipslop.
Slipslop Parson Adams.
Adams Ah, how is everything back at the Booby mansion?
Slipslop Mr Adams, there has been a strange alternation in our family.
Adams But why?
Slipslop Ever since the boy's departure . . .
Adams Boy? What boy?
Slipslop Why, her footman, naturally, Joseph Andrews. Ever since his departure, she hath behaved more like a mad woman than anything else.
Adams Ever since Joseph . . . But why?

Slipslop I am pledged not to talk about it. But I can whisper it.

She whispers in Adams's ear. He is aghast

Adams I am indeed concerned to find her ladyship behave in so unbecoming a manner. And with a lad, her own servant...

Joseph limps and staggers in from L. Around his neck is the ribbon with the piece of gold

Slipslop Joseph!
Joseph Mrs Slipslop. Parson, I know that our money is limited...
Adams None.

Mrs Tow-Wouse enters L, and hears this

Joseph So I think it best we move on, before we run up any more of a bill.
Mrs Tow-Wouse The bill. Yes, the bill must be paid.
Joseph We have nothing.
Mrs Tow-Wouse (*indicating the gold piece*) I cannot conceive a man could want money whilst he had gold to flaunt around his neck.
Joseph (*clutching it*) I have such a value of this little piece of gold that I would not part with it for a hundred times the riches which the greatest gentleman in the country is worth.
Mrs Tow-Wouse A pretty way indeed, to run to debt, and then refuse to part with your money, because you have value for it! I never knew any piece of gold of more value than as many shillings as it would change for.
Joseph Not to preserve my life from starving would I part with this dear piece!
Mrs Tow-Wouse (*belligerently*) I'll see that I get...
Adams Wait. Both of you. Calm yourselves. Mrs Tow-Wouse, is there no clergyman in this parish?
Mrs Tow-Wouse There is.
Adams Is he wealthy?
Mrs Tow-Wouse Rich? O yes.
Adams (*snapping his fingers*) Eureka, eureka!
Joseph Sir, what does that mean?
Adams In plain English, you need give yourselves no trouble. For I have a brother in the parish...
Mrs Tow-Wouse A brother? You have a brother here? Well...
Adams This brother will defray the reckoning. I will just step to his house and fetch the money and return to you instantly.
Joseph But sir, it is near evening, and it will be dark soon.
Adams Have no fear. I will be quick.

Adams exits R

Slipslop A rich clergyman. Madam, where did the rich clergyman get his money?

Act I

Mrs Tow-Wouse From his wife's pig farm.

Joseph, Slipslop and Mrs Tow-Wouse exit

The Scene becomes the countryside at dusk

Mrs Wilson enters L, to inform the audience of this. Adams enters R, trying to find his way

Mrs Wilson Parson Adams is not one of those people who can find his way to a place by instinct, or even directions. So he wanders a bit and night comes on while he is en route to the clergyman's house. And then . . .

Fanny is heard shrieking off. We do not know it is Fanny, and neither does Adams

Mrs Wilson exits L

Adams What is that? My Heavens, it sounds as if some damsel is in distress, great distress! I must hasten to the assistance of the poor creature whom some villains are murdering. (*He snaps his fingers*)

Fanny enters L fighting with Didapper, in the dimness. He throws her to the ground and almost overpowers her

Halt, I say.

Adams hits Didapper, who then turns to assail Adams, hitting him violently on the chest. They slug away at each other. Finally, Adams knocks Didapper down. He lies still—but is pretending, rather than unconscious

Be of good cheer, damsel. You are no longer in danger of your ravisher, who, I am terribly afraid, lies dead at my feet. But God forgive me what I have in defence of innocence. I wish he would stir. I should be concerned to have the blood of even the wicked on me.

Fanny (*trembling*) Thank you, sir, I guess. (*She shrinks from him*)

Adams Tell me by what misfortune you came, at such a time of night into so lonely a place.

Fanny I am travelling to an inn, and accidentally met with this ruffian from whom you delivered me. He offered to keep me company. I suspected no harm. Then, here, he desired me to stop. After some rude advances which I resisted, entreaties which I rejected, he laid violent hands on me, and was attempting to execute his wicked will, and I put my whole trust in Providence . . .

Adams I commend you for that.

Fanny I hope you have not delivered me from one rifler in order to rifle me yourself.

Adams No, no. You can . . .

They hear the Constable laughing and singing off

Fanny What is that? I fear . . .

Adams Be of good cheer, damsel, and repose your trust in the same Providence which hath hitherto protected thee, and never will forsake the innocent.

The Constable enters R, carrying a lantern

Constable Aye! (*Seeing Didapper laid out*) What's this?
Adams Who are you, sir?
Constable A constable of this county. The *law*.
Adams This man on the ground tried to—to attack this young damsel. Hold the lantern to his face, for I fear I have smote him fatally.

Before they can look at his face, Didapper leaps up and lays hold of Adams

Didapper No, villain, I am not dead. Though you and your whore——
Fanny O!
Didapper —might well think me so—after the barbarous cruelties you have exercised on me. (*To the Constable*) Sir, you are luckily come to the assistance of a poor traveller. I might otherwise have been robbed and murdered by this vile man and woman. They led me hither——
Fanny It is a lie!
Didapper —from off the high-road, and both fell on me, and used me as you see, hoping I had died and could not witness against them.
Constable Damn them! I will carry them both before the justice. (*He puts his lantern to Adam's face*) He has the most villainous countenance I have ever beheld.
Didapper He's a desperate fellow.
Constable I'll tie him up. Hold the lantern.

Didapper does so, and Adams, despite his protests, is tied back-to-back with Fanny. The Constable then examines Adams by his lantern

Adams O, if my friend Joseph Andrews was only here.
Fanny Sure I should know that voice. You cannot certainly, sir, be Mr Abraham Adams?
Adams Indeed, damsel, I am. There is something also in your voice which persuades me I have heard it before.
Fanny La, sir! Don't you remember poor Fanny?
Adams How, Fanny! Indeed I very well remember you.
Fanny I have heard of Joseph's misfortune.
Constable How, sirrah, do you go robbing in the dress of a clergyman? Let me tell you your habit will not entitle you to the benefit of clergy. Or else, you will have one benefit of clergy—(*making signs as if being hung by a noose*)—you will be exalted above the heads of the people.

Didapper runs off

Adams Wait! Constable, hold him.

Act I   21

Constable (*to Adams*) Stand you still.
Adams What else can I do? But your witness, so called, has escaped.
Fanny He was the villain.
Constable (*confounded*) We shall find out. I shall take you to the inn.

Fanny, Adams and the Constable exit R

The Scene shifts to the inn. Joseph is being besieged by Slipslop

Slipslop Sure, Joseph, you do not look yourself yet. If I could but take you to bed—I mean tuck you in . . .
Joseph I am well, Mrs Slipslop. I do think I should fare ill—in bed. Please excuse me.
Slipslop But Joseph, a little rest—a little bed rest . . .
Joseph I am not strong enough to rest. Pray, Mrs Slipslop, excuse me.
Slipslop (*hearing something off*) What's this racket?

Adams and Fanny enter R, *tied together, walking awkwardly, pushed in by the Constable*

Joseph Parson! Fanny! O my dearest! What . . .
Constable You know these two?
Joseph Yes. That is Parson Adams and . . .
Constable Parson? A real, truly clergyman?
Joseph Yes, one of the kindest men alive.
Constable (*untying them*) I owe you an apology, sir.
Adams (*trying to suppress his feeling*) Never mind. God bless you, and don't let it happen again, you imbecile.

The Constable exits R

Slipslop Parson Adams, I am sorry to see you in these circumstances.
Adams Mrs Slipslop, how do you do once more? Madam Slipslop, here—(*indicating Fanny*)—is one of your old acquaintance. Do but see what a fine woman she is grown since she left Lady Booby's service.
Slipslop I can't remember all the inferior servants in our family. I wonder, parson, that you are found in the company of that wench, who I fear is no better than she should be.
Adams I believe there is not a chaster damsel in the universe. I heartily wish, I heartily wish—(*snapping his fingers*)—that all her betters were as good. This poor maiden was almost ravished.
Fanny If Parson Adams hadn't smashed my ravisher—my *would-be* ravisher . . .
Slipslop (*to Adams*) I think you properer for the army than the clergy. It does not become a clergyman to lay violent hands on anyone.
Adams Fanny was about to be raped. What should I have done?
Slipslop Prayed that she might be strengthened. Joseph, I have told you how my ladyship bewails your absence. Will you return with me?
Joseph I cannot, Mrs Slipslop.

Slipslop Very well. I will inform my lady what doings were carrying on, and do not doubt but she will rid the parish of all such people.

Nose in air, Slipslop exits L

Fanny O Joseph, I will be yours for ever.
Joseph Parson, I beg you to instantly join our hands, our hearts, our bodies——
Fanny Joseph!
Joseph —together.

During Adams's speech, Joseph and Fanny almost consummate what is being discussed, with their hugging and groping

Adams I will by no means consent to anything contrary to the forms of the church. I have no licence. The church has prescribed a form—namely the publication of banns—with which all good Christians ought to comply, and to the omission of which I attribute the many miseries which befall great folks in marriage. (*Seeing what they are doing*) What are . . . Stop it! Instantly!
Fanny (*as they break apart*) I agree with the parson. I assure you, Joseph. I would not consent to any such thing, and I wonder at your offering it,
Adams It is almost light once more. I will off to see the Trullibers, as I intended last night. From my fellow clergyman, I will borrow the necessary funds. Try to get along without me.

Adams exits R

Joseph and Fanny have not heard Adams's farewell speech. They hold hands, look into each other's eyes

Joseph and Fanny exit

The scene changes to the Trulliber pig farm. There are pigs in the yard

Mrs Trulliber enters, in apron, and carrying a pail of slops. She is large and walks like a goose. When she speaks, it is loud. She looks off R

Mrs Trulliber O, he must be the dealer who is to come about the pigs. He has come in good time. They are all pure and fat and upwards of twenty score apiece. O, yes, I have often seen him at the fair. I remember his face very well, but I won't mention a word more till he has seen them.

Adams enters R

Adams Mrs Trulliber?
Mrs Trulliber That's me. Welcome.
Adams Thanks. What I came to see . . .
Mrs Trulliber Not just to see. Do but handle them. (*She indicates the pigs*)
Adams What?

Act I

Mrs Trulliber Do but handle them. Step in, friend. Thou art welcome to handle them, whether thou dost buy or no.
Adams But no, I—you misunderstand. What I . . .
Mrs Trulliber No words, but until you handle them—not one word.

She pushes Adams towards the pigs. Tentatively, at her urging, he takes hold of one of their tails. The unruly beast reacts badly to this and gives a sudden spring, which throws him in the mire

(*Contemptuously*) Why, does not thou know how to handle a hog?
Adams I am a clergyman, madam, and am not come to play with pigs.
Mrs Trulliber You came to see—
Adams Your husband.
Mrs Trulliber He is not at home.
Adams (*getting up and trying to make himself presentable*) I am a traveller. I was directed here, as your husband is a fellow clergyman.
Mrs Trulliber And one who could buy the vicar and the bishop both.
Adams Madam, I rejoice thereat. I request you to assist me with seven shillings. Three we owe and four we shall need on our journey. I shall return them to you. But if not, I am convinced you will joyfully embrace such an opportunity of laying up a treasure in a better place than any this world affords.
Mrs Trulliber Sire, we know where to lay up our little treasure as well as another. To be content with little is greater than to possess the world. Lay up our treasure! What matters where a man's treasure is whose heart is in the Scriptures? There is the treasure of a Christian.

Adams misunderstands. His eyes water with gratitude, and he catches her hand in rapture

Adams Sister, Heaven bless the accident that sent me to you. I would have walked many a mile to have communed with you. But, my friends will wonder why I tarry so long. So let me have the money immediately and I . . .
Mrs Trulliber Thou dost not intend to rob me?
Adams Rob? I?
Mrs Trulliber True. Thou are not a robber—but a beggar.
Adams Very true indeed.
Mrs Trulliber Seven shillings indeed! I won't give thee a farthing. I don't believe thou art a clergyman. But if thou art, thou deserve to have thy gown stript over thy shoulders for running about in such a manner.
Adams I am a clergyman, madam. But suppose I were not. I am nevertheless, thy brother, and thou as a Christian, much more as a clergyman's wife, art obliged to relieve my distress.
Mrs Trulliber Dost thou pretend to instruct me in my duty? I shall not learn my duty from such as thee. I know what charity is, better than to give to vagabonds. (*She starts to chase him with the pail of slops*)
Adams I am sorry that you do not know what charity is, since you practise it no better.

Adams exits R. *Mrs Trulliber throws the pail of slops at him just as he does so, then follows him*

The scene shifts to the inn

Joseph and Fanny enter L, *dreamily holding hands. They sit. Mrs Wilson enters* R, *then Betty enters* L

Betty glances jealously at the loving couple, then approaches Mrs Wilson

Betty Ma'am?
Mrs Wilson Ah—tea, please.
Betty Yes, ma'am.

Glaring at the couple, Betty exits L

Mrs Wilson watches Joseph and Fanny fondly

Adam enters R, *very discouraged*

Adams I have failed in my mission. (*He glances, then stares at Mrs Wilson*)
Fanny What should we do?
Joseph Let us ask the hostess to trust us.
Fanny I despair of that. She is one of the sourest women I have ever beheld.

Adams is still staring at Mrs Wilson. Joseph and Fanny are engrossed in each other

Adams Madam, do I not know you?
Mrs Wilson I believe so, parson. I am from the next parish.
Adams Mrs . . . ?
Mrs Wilson Wilson. The widow, Mrs Wilson.
Adams Of course. Now I recollect. Forgive me. You have isolated yourself, I believe.
Mrs Wilson Yes. I had a small fortune on my husband's death. I purchased a little place, whither I retired from the world.
Adams Ah yes.
Mrs Wilson The world—so full of bustle, noise, hatred, envy and ingratitude.
Adams And retired to . . .
Mrs Wilson To ease, quiet and love. But then, alas, soon after, I lost my son.
Adams O Mrs Wilson, we must submit to Providence, and consider death as common to all.
Mrs Wilson We must submit, indeed, and if he had died, I could have borne the loss.
Adams But you said . . .
Mrs Wilson Alas, sir, he was stolen away from my door by gypsies.

Act I

Adams By gypsies?
Mrs Wilson Poor child! He had the sweetest look. I ask your pardon, sir, for these tears.
Adams (*crying himself*) That is all right. I understand those—those gracious feminine feelings.

Mrs Tow-Wouse enters L with tray on which is a pot of tea, a cup, sugar and cream

Mrs Tow-Wouse Your tea, madam. The hostess of the inn does not think it beneath her dignity to serve the customers. (*She sets down the tray, and turns to Adams*) Did you get the money?
Adams I—well—you—I . . .
Mrs Tow-Wouse You didn't.
Adams Madam, will you trust us?
Mrs Tow-Wouse Why, of course.

The three are shocked

Fanny You will?
Mrs Tow-Wouse Surely. What do you take me for?
Joseph Well . . .
Fanny Hush, Joseph.
Adams We will be on our way then. By the by, Mrs Tow-Wouse, I got my coat dirty at the Trullibers. I am not anxious to renew my visit, so . . .
Mrs Tow-Wouse Ah, I will fetch it from your brother.
Fanny His brother?
Mrs Tow-Wouse Why, yes. When you set out, parson, you said he was your brother.
Adams O my dear hostess—brother in divinity, not natural brothers.
Mrs Tow-Wouse Not brothers? Then I could not get my money from them?
Adams From the Trullibers? Money? Might as well go to the kitchen and try to obtain blood from turnips.
Mrs Tow-Wouse Folks might be ashamed of travelling about, pretending to be what they are not.
Adams (*to Mrs Wilson*) Mrs Wilson, could I impose on you? Would you like to buy—or hold in pawn—a manuscript book of sermons? Or several books of sermons.
Mrs Wilson Why, yes, let me see them.
Adams (*to Joseph and Fanny*) Our troubles are over! (*He reaches under the table to get his back-pack*) Here, madam, here is a treasure of good writing about good works—a treasure, which will be my treasure. (*He reaches joyfully into the pack. As his hands search, his expression goes to puzzlement, wonderment, finally a bit despairing as he rummages faster and deeper*) I—what? What can . . . ? Is it possible? Who? There doesn't seem to be . . .

Adams pulls a bit of clothing from the bag. It is a pair of long underwear. Fanny blushes and turns away

Mrs Tow-Wouse Are those your sermons—underdrawers?
Joseph Sir, I don't understand.
Adams My wife—she must have thought I needed clean undergarments more than I need my sermons. She took them out and put these in.
Mrs Tow-Wouse And you wanted me to trust you for my bill—for underwear! I heard my own minister talk of sermons in stone, but not in underwear.
Mrs Wilson Pray, sir, put back your clothing. I need not your sermons to hold in pawn.
Adams Madam, I assure you, I meant no hoax.
Mrs Wilson No need to protest more, parson. I will pay your debts here.
Adams You will?
Joseph You will?
Mrs Tow-Wouse You will?
Mrs Wilson Yes.
Adams Bless you, Mrs Wilson.
Fanny Yes, madam, all our thanks.

Joseph goes to Mrs Wilson

Joseph Thank you. You have given us new life. (*He kisses her hand*)
Adams Without my sermons, there is no need to go to London. Let us, the three of us, Joseph, Fanny, head homeward.
Mrs Wilson (*taking out her purse to pay the hostess*) Go you three, on your way, on the road and may the Lord go with you.

Adams, Fanny and Joseph exit R, *saying "Good-bye, farewell" and the like*

Mrs Wilson follows to the edge of the stage to see them off. Mrs Tow-Wouse takes the coins and counts them

Mrs Wilson Do you think everything will go well for them?
Mrs Tow-Wouse Do you jest? Nothing but bad fortune will follow that bunch!

CURTAIN

ACT II

Mrs Wilson enters R. *Her words are acted out by Joseph, Fanny and Adams, who enter* L

Mrs Wilson Our friends, Joseph, Fanny and Parson Adams journey back with no money and less and less hope heading back to their home countryside. Hungry, and as night is coming on with no place to rest, they despair. Parson Adams leaves his two tired companions to speed ahead to the nearest large estate. It belongs to a friend of Lady Booby's, to a man by the name of Mr Didapper. *Man* did I say? Lecher, rather. And one we will find later who is not entirely unknown to poor unfortunate Fanny.

Mrs Wilson, Adams, Fanny and Joseph exit R

The Scene becomes Didapper's dining-room

Didapper enters L *and appears to be looking out of a window*

Adams enters R, *as the cordial supplicant*

Adams Sir . . .
Didapper Yes, what is it? You wanted to see the master of the house. That is me.
Adams Good evening, sir. I hope I'm not disturbing you.
Didapper That's past hoping for now.
Adams I see you observing the view. A fine view.
Didapper A fine view because it is my own. I only have delight in that kind of view—of my property. Otherwise, a fig for the view. But I am not looking at the view. I am expecting a guest—a widow, a *rich* widow. Pretty too. But first off, *rich*.
Adams Sir, I and my companions need help. We are travellers and . . .
Didapper I can give you directions to find your way.
Adams You don't understand, sir. We are not lost.
Didapper You must be, else why are you here asking directions?
Adams Sir, I am not. As I said, we want help—food, lodging, and perhaps a bit of cash to help us on our way.
Didapper Is this not the Didapper estate? Did you find a sign over the gate saying "Alms-House"? "Poor Farm"?
Adams No, sir, but you are obviously rich.
Didapper Tut, tut. Appearances are deceiving. You, as a preacher—if you are and not a beggar in a cassock—should know there are illusions, that one should not judge by the surface, that . . .

Adams Sir, I know you are rich. Riches are a blessing only to him who makes them a blessing to others.
Didapper Spoken like a poor man.
Adams Riches without charity is nothing worth.
Didapper Charity. I do not like the word. Charity. What is your idea of charity?
Adams My definition of charity is a generous disposition to relieve the distressed.
Didapper There is something in that definition which I like well enough. It is, as you say, a *disposition*, and does not so much consist in the act as in the disposition to do it. But alas, Mr Adams, who are the distressed? The distresses of mankind are mostly imaginary.
Adams Sure, sir, hunger and thirst, cold and nakedness, and other distresses which attend the poor, can never be said to be imaginary evils.
Didapper How can any person complain of hunger in a country where excellent salads are to be gathered in every field?
Adams Sir, you mean—weeds!
Didapper And complain of thirst, where every river produces abundant drink? As for cold and nakedness, a man by nature wants clothes no more than a horse does. There are whole nations who go without them.
Adams You will pardon me if I . . .
Didapper The greatest fault in our constitution is the provision made for the poor. I fancy, Mr Adams, from what you said that you imagine I am a lump of money.
Adams Well, yes.
Didapper Pray, where should I have gathered that vast quality of riches? Since I inherited nothing, where could I possibly have acquired such a treasure, unless I had stole it?
Adams Truly, I am of that same opinion.
Didapper (*insulted*) Sir! Leave my house. I will have none of you beggars in . . .

Fanny and Joseph enter R

Didapper (*enchanted by Fanny's beauty*) Pray, who is this?
Fanny I have the vague recollection I met you somewhere before, sir.
Didapper If so, how could I forget? I might forget a face, but not that . . .
Joseph Are you going to feed us?
Didapper Why don't you two fellows go to the kitchen and fill yourselves up. Please don't spare the liquor. It is my charity, parson.
Joseph She will come with us.
Fanny Yes, I will.
Didapper Spare her with me a few moments. Go, go and dine—drink plenty. I will give the young woman some wine and sweetmeats here till you return. But don't hurry.
Adams But why do you want to talk to Fanny?
Didapper I have a little something of import to import to her.
Joseph Fanny . . .

Act II

Didapper Go, or you'll all sleep in a ditch tonight.
Adams Come, Joseph. We are within hearing distance of any shouting.

Adams and Joseph exit L

Fanny What was it you wish to import to me, Mr Didapper?
Didapper Ah, you know my name—and I know yours. We are on the way to a nice intimacy.
Fanny You had something to import to me?
Didapper (*grabbing her*) Just this—my love for you.
Fanny Now I know you! You are the man who tried to assault me.
Didapper Me? Me assault you? Don't be silly. (*But he tries now to do just that*)
Fanny Parson Adams rescued me once, and he'll do it again.
Didapper (*letting go*) Yes, I remember the blow. For a preacher, he is a mighty pugilist. Still, I desire you.
Fanny I shall scream. I am contracted to Joseph.
Didapper That clod? (*The wily seducer*) Splendour and luxury will be yours. If you allowed me, Fanny, I could reveal love to you, I could be the instrument of such happiness, that you would despise that pitiful fellow. Only your ignorance could make you fond of him.
Fanny I was never fond of any pitiful fellow.
Didapper What better can be said of him? Notwithstanding your fondness for him.
Fanny I believe he is as honest a creature as any alive.
Didapper Honest? That proves it! Pitiful.
Fanny As for fondness for one of the opposite sex . . .
Didapper I warrant you, I shall find means to persuade you to be fond. Gad, but you are gorgeous. I love a pretty girl more than anything—except my own money—or the money of other people.

He grabs her again and tries to wrestle her to the couch. She screams, and they struggle

Joseph and Adams rush in L

They would like to grab and smash Didapper, but he manages to squirm out of their reach, and holds Fanny in front of him as a shield. She is too busy getting her clothes back in order, to escape

Didapper It was a mistake. You misunderstand. She misunderstands.
Joseph Are you all right, Fanny?
Didapper Of course she is. Nothing happened.
Adams She screamed.
Didapper She—she, ah, she saw a mouse and . . .
Adams A rat, you mean.

Joseph and Adams manage to grab Didapper and throw him down. They are about to pound on him

Mrs Booby enters R

Lady Booby What is going on?
Joseph Your ladyship!
Adams Lady Booby.
Didapper My visitor. Lady Booby, thank God you are come. These assassins . . .
Lady Booby I know them.
Didapper You do?
Lady Booby My former footman, Joseph Andrews, his—his paramour, I assume, Fanny Goodwill, and my parson.
Didapper (*feeling safe*) He called me a rat.
Adams And so you are. And worse.
Didapper If you were not a parson, I would not take these words. But your gown protects you. If any man who wears a sword had said so much, I had pulled him by the nose before this.
Adams If you attempted any such rudeness to my person, you would not find any protection for yourself in my gown. (*Clenching his fist*) I have thrashed many a stouter man.
Lady Booby (*to Adams*) I tell you, sir, it does not become a man of the cloth to run about the country with an idle fellow and a wench. You are doing a monstrous thing in endeavouring to provoke a match between these two.
Adams As for the young woman, I assure your ladyship I have as good an opinion of her as your ladyship herself.
Lady Booby (*affronted*) Ha!
Adams She is the sweetest-tempered, honestest, worthiest young creature. Indeed, as to her beauty . . .
Lady Booby You are very impertinent to talk such fulsome stuff to me. It is mighty becoming in a clergyman to trouble himself about handsome women. A country wench a beauty! I shall be sick whenever I hear beauty mentioned again.
Adams As for Mister Joseph Andrews . . .
Lady Booby Pray, don't *mister* such fellows to me. He is a vagabond. You and he and the great beauty may go and beg together I condemn my humility for demeaning myself to converse with you so long.
Adams We take our leave.
Didapper Take it and be damned.

Adams, Joseph, and Fanny exit R

Lady Booby I am resolved to have no discarded servants of mine settled here, in my neighbourhood.
Didapper The laws of this land are not so vulgar to permit a mean fellow to contend with one of your ladyship's name. Have him up before the law—before Justice Frolick. The judge, upon hearing your ladyship's name, will commit Joseph Andrews to prison, without any further questions.

Act II 31

Lady Booby Take what measures you please, good Mr Didapper. As for the ugly slut—you know, dear Mr Didapper, these forward creatures, who run after men, will always find some as forward as themselves.

They move to each other

So, to prevent the increase of beggars, we must get rid of Fanny Goodwill.

Lady Booby and Didapper exit L. *Mrs Wilson enters* R. *During her speech, Joseph and Fanny enter* R, *tied together, and led across the stage by the Constable*

Mrs Wilson And so Fanny and Joseph were arrested and taken to jail, to await an appearance before the stern judge, Justice Frolick.

Mrs Wilson exits R

The Scene becomes the Booby mansion

Slipslop enters L

Slipslop (*anxiously calling off* R) Your ladyship. Lady Booby. Your ladyship.

Lady Booby enters R

Lady Booby Stop that shouting. What is it, Slipslop? All this commotion!
Slipslop O ma'am, what does your ladyship think?
Lady Booby I don't think anything but that my ears are ringing.
Slipslop Joseph and Fanny are to be brought before the justice.
Lady Booby Is that what you bothered me about?
Slipslop All the parish are in tears.
Lady Booby Why?
Slipslop They say they will certainly be hanged—nobody knows what for.
Lady Booby I suppose they deserve it. What! Does thou mention such wretches to me?
Slipslop As for Fanny, I don't think it signifies much what becomes of her. But O, dear madam, is it not a pity such a graceless young man——
Lady Booby (*correcting her*) Graceful.
Slipslop —such a graceful young man should die a virulent death?

Nephew enters L

Lady Booby And what is it, Nephew, brings you to me?
Nephew My dear Aunt, I want you to be the first to know. She has accepted my proposal.
Lady Booby Who? What? What proposal? Who has accepted?
Nephew Why, my proposal of marriage—and to dear Pamela, of course.

Slipslop Pamela? Pamela Andrews?
Nephew Yes.
Lady Booby Joseph's sister?
Nephew Yes. Why are you . . . ?
Lady Booby O Lord! You will marry Pamela Andrews?
Nephew Yes, I will. Why are you so pale?
Slipslop She should faint.
Lady Booby I have sent Joseph—who is to be a relative—to prison.
Nephew You did what? Pamela's brother? Joseph!
Lady Booby You must act quickly to prevent this.
Nephew Yes, for our sake. (*As an afterthought*) For his, too, of course.

Nephew exits hurriedly L. *Lady Booby and Slipslop exit* R

The Scene changes to the chambers of Justice Frolick. This can be played in front of the CURTAIN *in a pool of light, if desired*

Justice Frolick enters L, *with Nephew*

Justice I have only ordered them to prison for a month.
Nephew Only—a month! What crime are they guilty of?
Justice Larceny. Ay, a kind of felonious larcenous thing. I believe I must order them a little correction, too. A little stripping and whipping— (*lecherously*)—especially a little stripping and whipping of that gorgeous —(*Breaking off*) Duty is duty.
Nephew Still, I am ignorant of the crime.
Justice (*showing a paper*) Why, here is the complaint.
Nephew Complaint by whom?
Justice A Mr Didapper, a friend of Lady Booby's.
Nephew I see. Well . . .
Justice (*reading*) "Between the hours of two and four in the afternoon, Joseph Andrews and Francis Goodwill"—Fanny . . .
Nephew Yes, I realize that. But . . .
Justice They did "walk across a certain field belonging to the complaintant"—Mr Didapper——
Nephew Yes, I understand, but . . .
Justice "—and there Joseph Andrews with a knife cut one twig, of the value of three half-pence or thereabouts."
Nephew A twig? Did I understand you to say "a twig"?
Justice Yes. "And the said Francis Goodwill was likewise walking on the grass of the said field, and did receive and carry in her hand the said twig, and so was comforting, aiding and abetting the said Joseph therein."
Nephew Jesu! Would you commit two persons to prison for a twig?
Justice Yes, and with great lenity too. For if we had called it a young tree, they would have been both hanged. (*Confidentially*) I believe Lady Booby desired to get them out of the parish.
Nephew I will take care that my aunt shall be satisfied in this point. I

Act II

shall be obliged to you, therefore, if, instead of prison, you will commit them to my custody.

Justice turns away from Nephew, but holds his hand back towards him for a bribe, and keeps talking until Nephew puts some money in his hand

Justice That is highly irregular, and without precedent, and against the standards of not only this court and myself, but the highest courts of law in all the nation, which ... (*He looks at the cash*) But, yes, to be sure, sir, if you desire it.

Justice and Nephew exit L

The Scene changes to the Booby mansion

Pamela, in her wedding dress, enters R, *followed by Joseph, who is nicely dressed*

Joseph Pamela, you look splendid.
Pamela I do, don't I? It took me so long to get a wedding gown, I may never wear anything else. Could you hear me in the church saying my vows?
Joseph I think they could hear you outside, you were so—so clear.
Pamela I earned this day. No bride ever worked harder—or held out so forthrightly.

Pamela and Joseph exit L. *Lady Booby and Slipslop enters* R, *in finery for the wedding*

Lady Booby Slipslop, what do you think of this wonderful creature my nephew has married?
Slipslop (*wondering which way she is expected to answer*) Madam, I ...
Lady Booby I ask you what you think of the dowdy niece—I think I am supposed to now call her my niece ...
Slipslop O yes, dowdy is the most praiseworthy thing you could say about such a plain, not to say homely, creature.
Lady Booby You do her more than justice. But yet, bad as she is, she is an angel ...
Slipslop (*thinking she had made a mistake in her condemnation*) O?
Lady Booby An angel, compared to Fanny.
Slipslop O my yes, Fanny. There is always something in those low-life creatures which must eternally extinguish them from their betters.
Lady Booby *Distinguish* them. But really, Slipslop, I think there is one exception to your rule. I am certain you may guess who I mean.
Slipslop (*unable to guess*) Well, I—of course, your ladyship, I ...
Lady Booby You are the dullest wretch. I mean a young fellow.
Slipslop O la! Yes, truly, madam, he is an accession.
Lady Booby An *exception*. Is he not so genteel that a prince might, without a blush, acknowledge him for his son? Such integrity, such bravery,

such goodness that, if he had been born a gentleman, his wife would have possessed the most invaluable blessing.

Slipslop To be sure, ma'am.

Lady Booby But as he is—I should despise myself for even thinking of him.

Slipslop To be sure, ma'am.

Lady Booby (*turning on her*) And why to be sure? Is he not more worthy of affection than an idle, worthless rake, though born of a family as old as the flood? And yet, to shun the contempt of one's equals, we must prefer title and fortune to real merit. We are the slaves of custom.

Slipslop Marry come up! If I was a woman of your ladyship's fortune and quality, I would be a slave to nobody.

Lady Booby Me? I am speaking if a young woman of fashion should happen to like such a fellow. Me, indeed! I hope thou dost not imagine . . .

Slipslop No, ma'am, no to be sure.

Lady Booby No! Why no? So far, I must allow he is a charming fellow. Me, indeed!

Slipslop Well, never tell me what people say, whilst I would be happy in the arms of him I love. Why should not your ladyship marry the brother as well as your nephew the sister?

Lady Booby So, if you were a woman of condition, you would really marry Mister Joseph Andrews.

Slipslop Yes, if he would have me.

Lady Booby Fool! *If* he would have a woman of fashion! Is that a question!

Slipslop It would be none if Fanny was out of the way.

Lady Booby True. Even if I could prevail on myself to commit such a weakness, there is that cursed girl in the way.

Slipslop Leave her to me.

Lady Booby What will you do.

Slipslop Discredit her.

Lady Booby How?

Slipslop How, madam? How else is a virgin discredited?

Lady Booby O! But who?

Slipslop You told me that one Mr Didapper is fond of her looks.

Lady Booby Fond? La!

Slipslop Send word to him to be a guest at the wedding supper. Leave the rest to me.

Slipslop exits R, *as Nephew enters* L

Nephew Aunt, may I have a word with you?

Lady Booby Yes. What about, pray?

Nephew Aunt, I have married a worthy woman, and I am resolved to own her relations.

Lady Booby You speak of Joseph Andrews?

Nephew Yes. I wish to show him and Mrs Andrews, the mother of both, all of them a proper respect.

Act II

Lady Booby (*pretending reluctance*) Well...
Nephew It is true that Joseph was your servant, but through this marriage, he has become my brother.
Lady Booby And since you beg this favour, as such I shall regard him. You know how easily I am prevailed on to do anything which Joseph Andrews desires of me. (*Catching her error*) I mean, of course, which *you* desire of me.
Nephew Also...
Lady Booby There's more?
Nephew There is a young woman...
Lady Booby (*warily*) Yes?
Nephew Her name is Fanny Goodwill and...
Lady Booby Don't impose on me, Nephew! Because I have so much condescended as to agree to suffer your brother-in-law, don't think I will submit to the company of all my former servants. Especially, of all the dirty trollops in the country...
Nephew My dear aunt, it is not for *my* sake.
Lady Booby Whose then?
Nephew Joseph asked.
Lady Booby Upon my soul, I resent this. I take even the request as an affront, much less admitting her—to... (*Thinking over Slipslop's plan*) But still, I am of all women the most tender-hearted and yielding to sympathy. I give in. She may stay here.
Nephew My dear aunt, I can't tell you how much this will mean to Joseph.
Lady Booby I will have someone see to her every desire. I will turn Fanny over to my own personal servant, Slipslop.

The stage fills with almost everyone in the cast, as they enter, from L *and* R, *for the wedding party: Joseph, Fanny, Pamela, Mrs Andrews, Adams, Mrs Wilson, Didapper*

(*To Mrs Andrews*) Mrs Andrews, you must be proud that your daughter has risen so high in the world as to marry my nephew.
Mrs Andrews As proud as he must be to have my Pamela.
Lady Booby (*scornfully*) Hmm.
Joseph My mother shall have more good news.
Mrs Andrews What is that, son?
Joseph I too am to be married.
Lady Booby You?
Joseph Yes. To a wonderful girl...
Nephew And a great beauty!
Lady Booby (*to Nephew*) I wonder that since you pretend that you married for love...
Nephew Pretend? I protest.
Lady Booby You think it proper to amuse the wife you love with *this* subject? For my part, my darling Pamela, I should be jealous of a husband who spoke so warmly in praise of another woman.

Pamela (*vainly*) La, I think this is an instance of my husband's aptness to see more beauty in a woman than she is mistress of.
Joseph I protest. My wonderful girl . . .
Lady Booby Men are, in general, very ill judges of beauty.
Fanny (*downcast*) I think I shall retire.
Lady Booby (*to Fanny*) Seek out Slipslop. She will show you which bed.
Joseph I will go with you.
Mrs Andrews Joseph!
Joseph I only meant—Mother, do you take me for a rake?

Fanny and Joseph exit L

Lady Booby (*to all*) You might perceive, in my condescension to admit my own servant to my table, that I look on that family of Andrews as relations. It will become all of you to endeavour by all methods to raise it as much as possible.
Mrs Andrews Fanny seems like a nice girl.
Pamela A nice farm girl.
Nephew What did you have in mind, dear aunt?
Lady Booby Use all your persuasion to get him to cast off Fanny. That being done, we might gain Joseph Andrews an alliance which will not be to our discredit.
Didapper Who?
Lady Booby La! We'll see.

Joseph enters L. *Lady Booby motions for the others to exit* R, *and all go, except Joseph, Nephew and Pamela*

Nephew Joseph . . .
Joseph Sir?
Pamela No longer "sir". He is now your brother.
Nephew And as such, I take the liberty of mentioning that which may be disagreeable to you to hear.
Joseph Which is?
Nephew If you have any value for my alliance or my friendship, you will decline any thoughts of engaging further with . . .
Pamela (*impatiently*) He means, give up Fanny.
Joseph What?
Nephew She is a girl who is, as you are now a relation of mine, so much beneath you.
Joseph (*threateningly*) Why you . . .
Pamela Calm yourself, brother. Be reasonable.
Nephew I own, indeed, she is handsome, but beauty alone is a poor ingredient for marriage.
Joseph Sir, I assure you that her beauty is her least perfection. Her virtues are so many that . . .
Pamela If she had never so many, Joseph, you will find her equal in those among her superiors in birth—and fortune.

Act II 37

Nephew Will you degrade yourself with such a match?
Joseph I am resolved to raise her as high above her present station as you have raised my sister.
Nephew There is a wide difference.
Joseph Which is?
Nephew My fortune enabled me to please myself.
Joseph My fortune enables me to please myself likewise, for all my pleasure is centred in Fanny.

Displeased, Pamela and Nephew exit R, *as Mrs Andrews enters* R

Joseph Mother, I will not have an easy moment until Fanny is absolutely mine. I will beg Parson Adams that I might be suffered to go fetch a licence.
Mrs Andrews Tonight? So late? It can't be done, Joseph.
Joseph Then first thing in the morning. The parson is staying here tonight. Tomorrow he will join that pure girl to me. My bride!
Mrs Andrews Why are you having uneasy moments?
Joseph I fear—I don't know exactly what I fear.

Mrs Andrews and Joseph exit L. *Slipslop and Didapper enter* R

Slipslop I will show you in which bedroom I have put her. But how . . . ?
Didapper I am an excellent mimic. With your help, I will get some of Joseph's clothes, and I will use Joseph's voice to gain my desires.
Slipslop And in that way, gain my lady's desires also.

Slipslop and Didapper exit L. *Lady Booby enters* R, *followed almost immediately by Adams*

Adams Your ladyship . . .
Lady Booby Yes, parson?
Adams Lady Booby, I took the liberty . . .
Lady Booby (*playfully*) La, parson, you can take no liberties with me.
Adams Madam, I took the liberty of inviting into your kitchen a gypsy.
Lady Booby A gypsy?
Adams Yes, she was at the door when I was in the kitchen——
Lady Booby —stuffing one more joint of beef in, eh, parson?
Adams Well, I do have a good appetite, the Lord be praised. Anyway, she is tired and hungry, and I had one of the cooks give her something to eat.
Lady Booby How did she find her way here? It is so dark tonight.
Adams She has been here before.
Lady Booby Indeed? I don't recall any gypsies here.
Adams I gather it was many, many years ago.
Lady Booby A gypsy? How exciting. I will have her tell my fortune later.

There is a commotion off L, *Didapper yelling in terror and Joseph doing the*

terrorizing. Didapper runs in L, *pursued by Joseph. Didapper hides behind Lady Booby. Adams restrains Joseph*

Adams Joseph!
Lady Booby What is going on? What is the meaning of this hullabaloo?
Joseph This dirty, sneaking rat, who pretends to be a man . . .
Adams Joseph. Temper.
Lady Booby Joseph, you are insulting Mister Didapper.
Joseph I will kill Mister Didapper!
Adams Joseph, for shame!
Didapper He attacked me, ma'am.
Joseph I would have attacked an army in the same cause.
Lady Booby What cause?
Joseph Madam, he met Fanny in the hallway, and he was rude.
Lady Booby What? I suppose he would have kissed the wench. And is a gentleman to be struck for such an offer? I must tell you, Joseph, these airs do not become you.
Adams I can commend him. I do not approve of killing, naturally, but Joseph is a brave lad, and it becomes any man to be the champion of the innocent.
Lady Booby (*lightly scornful*) Innocent? Fanny?
Joseph Yes, madam, innocent! She is as innocent as I am myself!
Adams He would be the basest coward who would not vindicate a woman with whom he is on the brink of marriage.
Lady Booby Parson Adams, you do not act in your proper character by encouraging such doings. We are violently set against this match, which is by no means suitable to our family.
Joseph I swear I will own no relation to anyone who is an enemy to her I love more than all the world.

Joseph rushes off L

Adams I must go to comfort the poor lad.

Adams exits L

Lady Booby Innocent? Didapper, take care of that.
Didapper I am obedient to your command, Lady Booby.

Didapper exits L. *Lady Booby* R

The Scene changes to the sleeping quarters of the Booby house. There are two beds. Fanny and Slipslop are asleep, Fanny in the bed R, *Slipslop* L, *but the audience does not know who they are. Adams, candle in hand, is saying good night to Joseph* L. *Both are in long night-shirts. Adams wears a nightcap*

Adams Try to sleep, Joseph.
Joseph I will, parson. But promise that first thing . . .

Act II

Adams Yes, yes, I will help you get the licence and . . .
Joseph And that lovely girl will be mine.
Adams Ah, Joseph, I like not this impatience. You seem to . . . Put carnal thoughts behind you, or someplace else. Try to sleep. Think of fields of flowers.
Joseph And being there with my dear Fanny.
Adams (*admonishing*) Joseph! Good night!

Joseph goes to his bed. Adams waits to see that he is there, then proceeds to go towards his bed. He is a bit foggy in the dark, and is turning around

Where am I here? Where's my room? All this talk with Joseph has made me hungry. I shall find my way to the kitchen. Just another little taste of beef.

Adams exits L. *Didapper, in nightwear and carrying a lighted candle, enters* R. *He goes to the door of Slipslop's room, speaking as he gets there*

Didapper This must be the room where Fanny is sleeping. (*He blows out the candle, and creeps to the bedside. Imitating Joseph's voice*) Fanny, my angel. It is me, Joseph. I am here to be your lover in deed as in word. I will not be delayed the enjoyment of you one moment longer. You could not say you love me if you deny me the possession of thy charms. (*He starts to embrace her*)
Slipslop What? Who . . . ?
Didapper You are not Fanny!
Slipslop (*holding him*) You shall not escape. Villain! You have attacked my chastity! I believe you ruined me in my sleep!
Didapper Let me go. It is I . . .
Slipslop I will swear out a rape against thee. I will prosecute thee with the utmost vengeance. (*As he struggles more violently*) Murder! Murder! Rape! Robbery! Ruin!

Adams rushes in L. *His candle goes out with the speed of his movement. He rushes to Slipslop's bed*

Adams I will rescue you, madam!

Didapper manages to break loose and escape R *as Adams grabs Slipslop, mistaking her for the assailant*

Slipslop (*hitting Adams*) That's for you.
Adams O, the rapist is tough, eh?
They fight
Adams Lights, lights here! I have captured a rapist! (*He holds her down*)

Lady Booby, with a lighted candle, enters R

I have him. Get the law. Lights!

Lady Booby What is going on, Slipslop?
Slipslop (*gasping*) O your ladyship—help!
Adams Slipslop?
Slipslop Help or I am ravished!
Adams (*realizing his mistake*) O my Lord! (*He lets her go*)
Lady Booby O, Parson Adams—you the wickedest of all men. The impudence of choosing my house for the scene of your debaucheries and my own woman for the object of your bestiality.
Adams I am disarrayed. (*He jumps into bed with Slipslop*)
Slipslop What are you doing?
Lady Booby Parson!
Adams I am covering my nakedness.
Slipslop Get out, get out!
Adams I am innocent. (*To Slipslop*) I ask ten thousand pardons for the blows I struck you—I mistook you for a witch.
Slipslop (*insulted*) O, to add insult to injury! O I have been so terrified!
Adams I heard her scream, my lady, and came to her rescue. I mistook Slipslop for the assailant.
Lady Booby Parson, you had best return to your bed as soon as I depart. I wish to see no naked men of your age.

Lady Booby exits R

Adams O Mrs Slipslop, please pardon me.
Slipslop (*more than forgiving*) O parson, I am of a most Christian temper. I not only forgive, but . . .

To her frustration, as she moves towards him, Adams gets up and heads to his own bed. Mistakenly, he goes into Fanny's room. He creeps in her bed with a sigh, and falls asleep. Joseph gets up and goes to Fanny's door and knocks twice

Joseph (*in a low voice*) Fanny. Fanny, we must plan for the morrow—and our wedding!
Adams (*sleepily*) What . . . ? Who . . . ? Come in, whoever you are.
Joseph (*startled*) What? What's this? Who . . . ? In Fanny's room!
Fanny (*awakening*) O heavens! Where am I? Who . . . ?
Adams Bless me! Where am I?

Fanny screams. Joseph is stunned as Adams jumps out of bed

Adams How came she into my room?
Joseph Your . . . How came you into hers?
Adams I know nothing of the matter. As I am a Christian, I know not whether she is a man or a woman. He is an infidel that does not believe in witchcraft. My clothes were bewitched away too, and Fanny's brought into their place. This is my room.
Fanny It is not so.
Adams It isn't!

Act II

Joseph Fanny, I know my friend Parson Adams well. He was no doubt confused in the dark.
Adams Fanny, I beg your pardon.
Fanny You are forgiven. I believe what you say. But please get out of my bed, parson. And both of you leave. I will get my clothes on again. I cannot sleep now.

Joseph and Adams exit L

The Scene changes to the parlour of the house

Pamela, Nephew and the Gypsy enter R

Nephew I have sent for Fanny.
Pamela You believe this gypsy's story?
Nephew It has several facts to it which make it sound not only plausible, but likely!

Lady Booby enters R

Lady Booby Has this household gone completely insane? Is everybody up and moving? You two—you—on your wedding night!
Nephew My dear aunt, this is the gypsy I told you of.
Lady Booby The middle of the night and you are entertaining a gypsy woman in my parlour?
Nephew Her conscience has troubled her. There is a guilt she must clear herself of.
Lady Booby What? I . . .
Gypsy Where is the girl who is called Fanny?
Lady Booby Fanny? What of her?

Fanny enters L, *followed by Joseph and Adams*

Gypsy You are Fanny?
Fanny (*puzzled*) Yes?
Lady Booby Any of us could have told you what her name is.
Gypsy I believe I can acquaint you with your parents.
Fanny My—my parents! You can!
Gypsy Years ago, we gypsies made a practice of stealing away children. It is almost impossible to describe the beauty of the young creature—about a year and half old when we kidnapped it—you. You, Fanny. We kept you about two years, when I sold you for three guineas to Sir Thomas Booby.
Lady Booby I wish I had the three guineas back.
Adams The child is Fanny—but who did you steal her from? What family?
Gypsy Their name was Andrews.

Everyone is thunderstruck

Joseph Andrews!
Pamela My Lord!
Adams It is a common name in this part of the country. I will fetch—Mrs Andrews!

Adams exits L. *Didapper enters* R

Pamela I cannot believe it. I never heard my mother had lost any child, or that she had any more than Joseph and myself.
Lady Booby Upstart! How dare you disown a relation who had so lately been on a level with you—a *lower* level.
Nephew If this young woman be proved her sister, we will readily embrace her as such.

Slipslop enters R

Pamela I have never heard my parents mention such an accident. It must certainly be false.
Lady Booby I'm sure it is true.
Joseph I earnestly wish it is false.
Nephew Mrs Andrews will soon be here. Then we shall know the truth or falsehood of this relation.
Pamela Still, Joseph, I think you should be chid for the concern which you express at discovering a new sister. If you love Fanny as you ought, with a pure affection, you have no reason to lament being related to her.
Didapper (*sardonically*) Yes, there is something strong and wonderful about Platonic love. The love that has no physical, earthly matter in it. It is like the non-corporal joy of the next world. I conclude that there is no such thing as real pleasure in this world.
Slipslop (*during Didapper's speech*) La! You'd think you was the preacher!

Pamela and Nephew smile and move closer. They become so enrapt with each other, they forget others are there

Lady Booby Where did that family live?
Gypsy About thirty miles from here.
Joseph O no. I...
Pamela Joseph, there are many Andrews in this part of the country.
Gypsy You will be sure to find out by one circumstance.
Lady Booby Which is?
Gypsy They had a daughter of a very strange name.
Pamela Strange? How?
Gypsy Some pronounced it one way, some the other—Pam-ella, or Pa-mel-a, or...
Joseph O God!
Fanny Joseph! My brother!
Lady Booby Thank heaven that this discovery has been made before the dreadful sin has been committed.

Act II   43

Fanny O yes, we are thankful. (*She cries*)
Joseph O my fate! Let me die here.
Pamela Don't talk that way.
Nephew Face it bravely, brother.
Lady Booby (*wryly*) Brother? We all seem to be brother and sister.
Fanny (*to Joseph*) If we find ourselves to be really brother and sister, my dear Joseph, let us vow perpetual celibacy, and live together all our days, and indulge a Platonic friendship for each other.
Didapper Will this night's wonders ever cease?

Adams enters L, with Mrs Andrews and Mrs Wilson

Nephew My dear lady, you have a child in this company more than you know of. (*Taking Fanny by the hand*) This is the daughter of yours who was stolen away by gypsies in her infancy

Stunned, Mrs Andrews does not move. Will she laugh at such an absurd notion? Will she be scornful? But no. It is true! Tears break out and she embraces Fanny

Mrs Andrews She is! She is my child.

Joseph goes pale

Joseph How . . . ? What . . . ?
Pamela Yes, mother, please explain this.
Mrs Andrews One afternoon, when this child was about a year old, two gypsy women came to the door . . .
Gypsy I was one of them. Please forgive me and I can die happy.
Mrs Andrews I left my daughter in the cradle and went to get a cup of water for the women.
Gypsy I remember. O . . .
Mrs Andrews I was not absent longer than the time it is taking me to say this, but when I returned the women were gone. I heard the child cry in the cradle. I went to take her up—but O! Instead of my little girl, who was a fat, thriving child, there was a poor, sickly boy. That poor infant our Joseph here, as stout as he now stands, lifted up his eyes upon me so piteously that as true as I am alive, I soon loved him all to nothing, as if he had been my own.
Gypsy Did not that child have on its breast a mark?
Mrs Andrews Yes, he had as fine a strawberry as ever grew in a garden.
Joseph It's true (*He unbuttons his shirt to show them*)
Mrs Wilson Joseph . . .
Joseph Mrs Wilson?
Mrs Wilson Joseph, may I see the mark? (*Seeing it, she embraces him with tears*) My son. I have discovered my son. I have him again in my arms.
Joseph I—*your* son?
Pamela Mrs Wilson—Joseph's mother!
Gypsy We stole that boy from a gentlewoman's house. We kept him a

whole year. We looked upon him as in a dying condition, and exchanged him for the other, healthier child.

At this point, almost everybody introduces everybody else—"my mother", "my son", etc. Didapper moves to Lady Booby and begins to fondle her

Mrs Wilson (*looking out at the audience*) The story is over. Have a good evening [or good day].

Amid the increasing hubbub—

the CURTAIN *falls*

FURNITURE AND PROPERTY LIST

NOTE: The following list includes the basic requirements for the various scenes. The author's suggestions should be studied regarding the various changes

ACT I

On stage: BOOBY PARLOUR
Settee
3 or 4 small chairs
Occasional table

INN
Bar. *On it:* glasses, bottles
2 or 3 benches
Inn sign

INN BEDROOM
Bed and bedding

DAIRY
Milking-stool (*optional*)

PIG FARM
Enclosure for pigs

Off stage: Prayerbook **(Lady Booby)**
Tray with decanter of wine and large glass **(Fanny)**
Small bundle of belongings **(Joseph)**
Old-fashioned hand-gun **(Male Robber)**
Back-pack containing clothes, including long underwear **(Adams)**
Bedwarming-pan **(Betty)**
Milk-pail **(Fanny)**
Lighted lantern **(Constable)**
Length of rope **(Constable)**
Club (*optional*) **(Constable)**
Pail of slops **(Mrs Trulliber)**
Tray with pot of tea, cup, cream, sugar **(Mrs Tow-Wouse)**

Personal: **Joseph:** coins
Fanny: ribbon with small piece of gold attached
Adams: cane (*optional*)
Mrs Wilson: purse with coins

ACT II

On stage: DIDAPPER'S DINING-ROOM
Table
1 or 2 chairs
Couch

BOOBY MANSION
as Act I

BOOBY SLEEPING-QUARTERS
2 beds with bedding and canopies

Off stage: Piece of paper with Indictment **(Justice)**
Lighted candle in holder **(Adams)**
Lighted candle in holder **(Didapper)**
Lighted candle in holder **(Lady Booby)**

Personal: **Nephew:** coins

LIGHTING PLOT

Property fittings required: nil
Various interior and exterior settings

ACT I
To open:	Spot on **Mrs Wilson**	
Cue 1	**Mrs Wilson:** "... a servant, Pamela."	(Page 1)
	Cross-fade to general lighting on parlour	
Cue 2	**Mrs Wilson:** "... in search of a bright future."	(Page 10)
	Cross-fade to dim Spot indicating a road	
Cue 3	**Betty** leads **Joseph** to inn	(Page 11)
	Cross-fade to general lighting on inn	
Cue 4	**Betty** and **Mrs Tow-Wouse** exit	(Page 15)
	*Concentrate lightning on **Joseph**'s bed*	
Cue 5	**Joseph** collapses on bed	(Page 16)
	Cross-fade to dairy lighting	
Cue 6	**Pamela** exits	(Page 16)
	Cross-fade to inn lighting	
Cue 7	**Mrs Tow-Wouse:** "... his wife's pig farm."	(Page 19)
	Cross-fade to dim countryside lighting, effect of dusk	
Cue 8	**Constable:** " ... take you to the inn."	(Page 21)
	Cross-fade to inn lighting	
Cue 9	**Joseph** and **Fanny** exit	(Page 22)
	Cross-fade to pig farm lighting	
Cue 10	**Mrs Trulliber** throws pail at **Adams**	(Page 24)
	Cross-fade to inn lighting	

ACT II
To open:	Spots on **Mrs Wilson** and the **Travellers**	
Cue 11	**Mrs Wilson:** "... to poor unfortunate Fanny."	(Page 27)
	Cross-fade to Didapper's dining-room	
Cue 12	**Lady Booby:** "... rid of Fanny Goodwill."	(Page 31)
	*Fade to Spot on **Mrs Wilson**: on her exit bring up Booby parlour lighting to full*	
Cue 13	**Lady Booby** and **Slipslop** exit	(Page 32)
	*Fade to pool of light for chambers of **Justice Frolick***	
Cue 14	**Didapper:** "... obedient to your command, Lady Booby."	(Page 38)
	Cross-fade to sleeping quarters of Booby house, very dim general lighting	
Cue 16	**Joseph** and **Adams** exit	(Page 41)
	Cross-fade to Booby parlour—full general lighting	

www.ingramcontent.com/pod-product-compliance
Ingram Content Group UK Ltd.
Pitfield, Milton Keynes, MK11 3LW, UK
UKHW021848210426
5322IPUK00022B/532